This Book Belong To :

_____

Ramadan Journal & Planner by AL-AMAL JOURNALS

Copyright © 2022 AL-AMAL JOURNALS

Cover by H.Ouahmane.

Printed in The Country Where Ordered

First Edition

Ramadan Days Tracker

1	2	3	4	5	6
7	8	9	10	11	12
13	14	15	16	17	18
19	20	21	22	23	24
25	26	27	28	29	30

PROPHET MUHAMMAD (ﷺ) SAID:

"When Ramadan begins, the gates
of Jannah are opened,
the gates of Hell are closed,
and the devils are chained."

(Al-Bukhari and Muslim)

Du'a after breaking the fast

ذَهَبَ الظَّمَأُ وَابْتَلَّتِ الْعُرُوقُ وَثَبَتَ الْأَجْرُ إِنْ شَاءَ اللَّهُ

**Dhahabaẓ-ẓama',
wabtallati 'l-ʿurūq,
wa thabata 'l-'ajru in shā Allāh.**

**Thirst has gone, the arteries are moist,
and the reward is sure, if God wills**

My Quran Reading Schedule

Day	Juz/Surah	From Ayah	To Ayah
1			
2			
3			
4			
5			
6			
7			
8			
9			
10			
11			
12			
13			
14			
15			
16			
17			
18			
19			
20			
21			
22			
23			
24			
25			
26			
27			
28			
29			
30			

Date _____

Ramadan Day 1

Mood

○ HAPPY   ○ OKAY

○ INSPIRED   ○ TIRED

○ PEACEFUL   ○ ANGRY

Du'a of the Day

رَبَّنَآ ءَاتِنَا فِى ٱلدُّنْيَا حَسَـنَةً وَفِى ٱلْأَخِرَةِ حَسَـنَةً وَقِنَا عَذَابَ ٱلنَّارِ

(البقرة: 201)

Rabbanā Ātinā Fī L-Dun'yā Ĥasanatan WaFī L-Ākhirati Ĥasanatan WaQinā `Adhāba L-Nāri

(Al-Baqarah: 201)

Our Lord! Grant us the good of this world and the Hereafter, and protect us from the torment of the Fire.

Reflection _____

_____

_____

_____

_____

_____

_____

Salah Tracker

FAJR
S 2 · F 2

DHUHR
S 4 · F 4 · S 2 · N 2

ASR
S 4 · F 4

MAGHRIB
F 3 · S 2 · N 2

ISHA'A
S 4 · F 4 · S 2 · N 2 · W 3 · N 2

TARAWIH
S 2 · S 2 · S 2 · S 2 · S 2 · S 2 · S 2 · S 2

Today's Deeds

○ QURAN
_____

○ DUAS
_____

○ KIND ACTION
_____

○ SADAQA
_____

○ GOOD SPEECH
_____

○ NIGHT PRAYER
_____

Tomorrow's Ramadan Goal

_____
_____
_____
_____
_____

Quran Study

before		after
start: surah .... ayah .... finish: surah .... ayah	**FAJR**	start: surah .... ayah .... finish: surah .... ayah ....
start: surah .... ayah .... finish: surah .... ayah	**DHUHR**	start: surah .... ayah .... finish: surah .... ayah ....
start: surah .... ayah .... finish: surah .... ayah	**ASR**	start: surah .... ayah .... finish: surah .... ayah ....
start: surah .... ayah .... finish: surah .... ayah	**MAGHRIB**	start: surah .... ayah .... finish: surah .... ayah ....
start: surah .... ayah .... finish: surah .... ayah	**ISHA'A**	start: surah .... ayah .... finish: surah .... ayah ....

Reflection

_____
_____
_____
_____
_____
_____
_____
_____
_____

Applecation

_____
_____
_____
_____
_____

To Do List

- [ ] _____
- [ ] _____
- [ ] _____
- [ ] _____
- [ ] _____
- [ ] _____
- [ ] _____
- [ ] _____

Meal Planner

SAHUR	IFTAR	DINNER
_____	_____	_____
_____	_____	_____
_____	_____	_____
_____	_____	_____
_____	_____	_____
_____	_____	_____
_____	_____	_____
_____	_____	_____
_____	_____	_____

Water Tracker

Adequate Daily Fluid Intake is:

15.5 cups (3.7 liters) a day for men

11.5 cups (2.7 liters) a day for women

Date _____

Ramadan Day 2

Fasting
- ○ YES
- ○ NO

Mood

- ○ HAPPY
- ○ INSPIRED
- ○ PEACEFUL
- ○ OKAY
- ○ TIRED
- ○ ANGRY

Du'a of the Day

رَبَّنَآ أَفۡرِغۡ عَلَيۡنَا صَبۡرًا وَثَبِّتۡ أَقۡدَامَنَا وَٱنصُرۡنَا عَلَى ٱلۡقَوۡمِ ٱلۡكَٰفِرِينَ

(البقرة: 250)

Rabbanā Afrigh `Alaynā Şabran WaThabbit Aqdāmanā Wa-unşur'nā `Alā L-Qawmi L-Kāfirīna

(Al–Baqarah: 250)

Our Lord! Shower us with perseverance, make our steps firm, and give us victory over the disbelieving people.

Reflection _____

_____

_____

_____

_____

_____

Salah Tracker

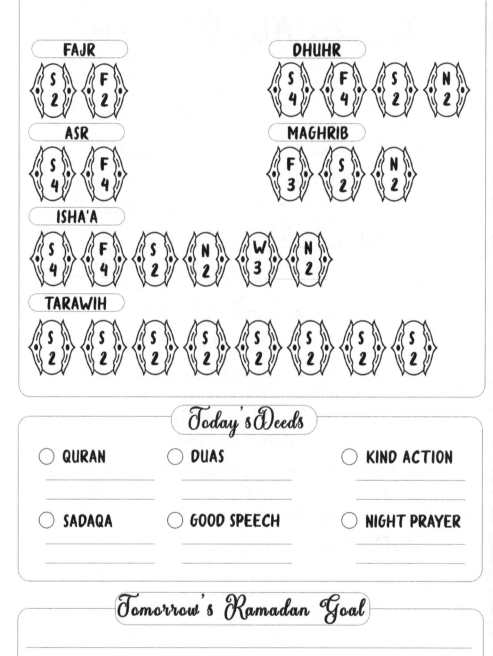

FAJR
- S 2
- F 2

DHUHR
- S 4
- F 4
- S 2
- N 2

ASR
- S 4
- F 4

MAGHRIB
- F 3
- S 2
- N 2

ISHA'A
- S 4
- F 4
- S 2
- N 2
- W 3
- N 2

TARAWIH
- S 2
- S 2
- S 2
- S 2
- S 2
- S 2
- S 2
- S 2

Today's Deeds

- ○ QURAN
  _____
  _____
- ○ DUAS
  _____
  _____
- ○ KIND ACTION
  _____
  _____
- ○ SADAQA
  _____
  _____
- ○ GOOD SPEECH
  _____
  _____
- ○ NIGHT PRAYER
  _____
  _____

Tomorrow's Ramadan Goal

_____
_____
_____
_____
_____

Quran Study

before		after
start: surah .... ayah .... finish: surah .... ayah	**FAJR**	start: surah .... ayah .... finish: surah .... ayah ....
start: surah .... ayah .... finish: surah .... ayah	**DHUHR**	start: surah .... ayah .... finish: surah .... ayah ....
start: surah .... ayah .... finish: surah .... ayah	**ASR**	start: surah .... ayah .... finish: surah .... ayah ....
start: surah .... ayah .... finish: surah .... ayah	**MAGHRIB**	start: surah .... ayah .... finish: surah .... ayah ....
start: surah .... ayah .... finish: surah .... ayah	**ISHA'A**	start: surah .... ayah .... finish: surah .... ayah ....

Reflection

_____
_____
_____
_____
_____
_____
_____
_____
_____

Applecation

_____
_____
_____
_____
_____
_____

To Do List

- [ ] _____
- [ ] _____
- [ ] _____
- [ ] _____
- [ ] _____
- [ ] _____
- [ ] _____
- [ ] _____

Meal Planner

SAHUR	IFTAR	DINNER

Water Tracker

Adequate Daily Fluid Intake is:

15.5 cups (3.7 liters) a day for men

11.5 cups (2.7 liters) a day for women

Ramadan Day 3

Mood

○ HAPPY ○ OKAY

○ INSPIRED ○ TIRED

○ PEACEFUL ○ ANGRY

Du'a of the Day

رَبَّنَا لَا تُزِغْ قُلُوبَنَا بَعْدَ إِذْ هَدَيْتَنَا وَهَبْ لَنَا مِن لَّدُنكَ رَحْمَةً إِنَّكَ أَنتَ ٱلْوَهَّابُ

(آل عمران:8)

**Rabbanā Lā Tuzigh Qulūbanā Ba`da
idh Hadaytanā WaHab Lanā Min Ladunka
Raĥmatan ّ innaka Anta L-Wahābu**

(Ali'imran :8)

Our Lord! Do not let our hearts deviate after you have guided us. Grant us Your mercy. You are indeed the Giver ˹of all bounties˺

Reflection _____

Salah Tracker

FAJR
S 2 | F 2

DHUHR
S 4 | F 4 | S 2 | N 2

ASR
S 4 | F 4

MAGHRIB
F 3 | S 2 | N 2

ISHA'A
S 4 | F 4 | S 2 | N 2 | W 3 | N 2

TARAWIH
S 2 | S 2 | S 2 | S 2 | S 2 | S 2 | S 2 | S 2

Today's Deeds

○ QURAN

_____

○ SADAQA

_____

○ DUAS

_____

○ GOOD SPEECH

_____

○ KIND ACTION

_____

○ NIGHT PRAYER

_____

Tomorrow's Ramadan Goal

_____

_____

_____

_____

_____

Quran Study

before		after
start: surah .... ayah .... finish: surah .... ayah	**FAJR**	start: surah .... ayah .... finish: surah .... ayah ....
start: surah .... ayah .... finish: surah .... ayah	**DHUHR**	start: surah .... ayah .... finish: surah .... ayah ....
start: surah .... ayah .... finish: surah .... ayah	**ASR**	start: surah .... ayah .... finish: surah .... ayah ....
start: surah .... ayah .... finish: surah .... ayah	**MAGHRIB**	start: surah .... ayah .... finish: surah .... ayah ....
start: surah .... ayah .... finish: surah .... ayah	**ISHA'A**	start: surah .... ayah .... finish: surah .... ayah ....

Reflection

_____
_____
_____
_____
_____
_____
_____
_____

Applecation

_____
_____
_____
_____
_____

To Do List

- ☐ _____
- ☐ _____
- ☐ _____
- ☐ _____
- ☐ _____
- ☐ _____
- ☐ _____
- ☐ _____

Meal Planner

SAHUR	IFTAR	DINNER

Water Tracker

Adequate Daily Fluid Intake is:

15.5 cups (3.7 liters) a day for men

11.5 cups (2.7 liters) a day for women

Date _____

Ramadan Day 4

Mood

○ HAPPY   ○ OKAY

○ INSPIRED   ○ TIRED

○ PEACEFUL   ○ ANGRY

Du'a of the Day

رَبَّنَآ إِنَّنَآ ءَامَنَّا فَٱغۡفِرۡ لَنَا ذُنُوبَنَا

وَقِنَا عَذَابَ ٱلنَّارِ

(آل عمران:16)

**Rabbanā innanā āmannā Fa-igh'fir Lanā
Dhunūbanā WaQinā `Adhāba L-Nāri**

(Ali'imran :16)

Our Lord! We have believed, so forgive our sins
and protect us from the torment of the Fire.

Reflection _____

_____

_____

_____

_____

_____

_____

Salah Tracker

FAJR
S2 · F2

DHUHR
S4 · F4 · S2 · N2

ASR
S4 · F4

MAGHRIB
F3 · S2 · N2

ISHA'A
S4 · F4 · S2 · N2 · W3 · N2

TARAWIH
S2 · S2 · S2 · S2 · S2 · S2 · S2 · S2

Today's Deeds

○ QURAN
_____
_____

○ DUAS
_____
_____

○ KIND ACTION
_____
_____

○ SADAQA
_____
_____

○ GOOD SPEECH
_____
_____

○ NIGHT PRAYER
_____
_____

Tomorrow's Ramadan Goal

_____
_____
_____
_____
_____

Quran Study

before		after
start: surah .... ayah .... finish: surah .... ayah	**FAJR**	start: surah .... ayah .... finish: surah .... ayah ....
start: surah .... ayah .... finish: surah .... ayah	**DHUHR**	start: surah .... ayah .... finish: surah .... ayah ....
start: surah .... ayah .... finish: surah .... ayah	**ASR**	start: surah .... ayah .... finish: surah .... ayah ....
start: surah .... ayah .... finish: surah .... ayah	**MAGHRIB**	start: surah .... ayah .... finish: surah .... ayah ....
start: surah .... ayah .... finish: surah .... ayah	**ISHA'A**	start: surah .... ayah .... finish: surah .... ayah ....

Reflection

_____

_____

_____

_____

_____

_____

_____

_____

Applecation

_____

_____

_____

_____

_____

To Do List

- [ ] _____
- [ ] _____
- [ ] _____
- [ ] _____
- [ ] _____
- [ ] _____
- [ ] _____
- [ ] _____

Meal Planner

SAHUR	IFTAR	DINNER

Water Tracker

Adequate Daily Fluid Intake is:

15.5 cups (3.7 liters) a day for men

11.5 cups (2.7 liters) a day for women

Date _____

Ramadan Day 5

Mood

○ HAPPY   ○ OKAY

○ INSPIRED   ○ TIRED

○ PEACEFUL   ○ ANGRY

Du'a of the Day

رَبِّ هَبْ لِى مِن لَّدُنكَ ذُرِّيَّةً طَيِّبَةً إِنَّكَ سَمِيعُ ٱلدُّعَآءِ

(آل عمران: 38)

**Rabbi Hab Lī Min Ladunka Dhurriyyatan
Ţayyibatanᵘ innaka
Samī`u L-Du`āi**

(Ali'imran :38)

My Lord! Grant me—by your grace—righteous
offspring. You are certainly
the Hearer of ʿallʾ prayers.

Reflection _____

_____

_____

_____

_____

_____

_____

Salah Tracker

FAJR

S 2 · F 2

DHUHR

S 4 · F 4 · S 2 · N 2

ASR

S 4 · F 4

MAGHRIB

F 3 · S 2 · N 2

ISHA'A

S 4 · F 4 · S 2 · N 2 · W 3 · N 2

TARAWIH

S 2 · S 2 · S 2 · S 2 · S 2 · S 2 · S 2 · S 2

Today's Deeds

○ QURAN

_____
_____

○ DUAS

_____
_____

○ KIND ACTION

_____
_____

○ SADAQA

_____
_____

○ GOOD SPEECH

_____
_____

○ NIGHT PRAYER

_____
_____

Tomorrow's Ramadan Goal

_____
_____
_____
_____
_____

Quran Study

before		after
start: surah .... ayah .... finish: surah .... ayah	**FAJR**	start: surah .... ayah .... finish: surah .... ayah ....
start: surah .... ayah .... finish: surah .... ayah	**DHUHR**	start: surah .... ayah .... finish: surah .... ayah ....
start: surah .... ayah .... finish: surah .... ayah	**ASR**	start: surah .... ayah .... finish: surah .... ayah ....
start: surah .... ayah .... finish: surah .... ayah	**MAGHRIB**	start: surah .... ayah .... finish: surah .... ayah ....
start: surah .... ayah .... finish: surah .... ayah	**ISHA'A**	start: surah .... ayah .... finish: surah .... ayah ....

Reflection

_____
_____
_____
_____
_____
_____
_____
_____
_____

Applecation

_____
_____
_____
_____
_____
_____

To Do List

- [ ] _____
- [ ] _____
- [ ] _____
- [ ] _____
- [ ] _____
- [ ] _____
- [ ] _____
- [ ] _____

Meal Planner

SAHUR	IFTAR	DINNER
_____	_____	_____
_____	_____	_____
_____	_____	_____
_____	_____	_____
_____	_____	_____
_____	_____	_____
_____	_____	_____
_____	_____	_____
_____	_____	_____

Water Tracker

Adequate Daily Fluid Intake is:

15.5 cups (3.7 liters) a day for men

11.5 cups (2.7 liters) a day for women

Date _____

Ramadan Day 6

Mood

○ HAPPY   ○ OKAY

○ INSPIRED   ○ TIRED

○ PEACEFUL   ○ ANGRY

Du'a of the Day

رَبَّنَآ ءَامَنَّا بِمَآ أَنزَلْتَ وَ ٱتَّبَعْنَا ٱلرَّسُولَ فَٱكْتُبْنَا مَعَ ٱلشَّـٰهِدِينَ

(آل عمران: 53)

Rabbanā Āmannā Bimā Anzalta
Wa-ittaba`nā L-Rasūla
Fa-uk'tub'nā Ma`a L-Shāhidīna

(Ali'imran :53)

Our Lord! We believe in Your revelations and follow
the messenger, so count us among those
who bear witness.

Reflection _____

_____

_____

_____

_____

_____

_____

Salah Tracker

FAJR
S2 F2

DHUHR
S4 F4 S2 N2

ASR
S4 F4

MAGHRIB
F3 S2 N2

ISHA'A
S4 F4 S2 N2 W3 N2

TARAWIH
S2 S2 S2 S2 S2 S2 S2 S2

Today's Deeds

○ QURAN

○ DUAS

○ KIND ACTION

_____

_____

_____

○ SADAQA

○ GOOD SPEECH

○ NIGHT PRAYER

_____

_____

_____

Tomorrow's Ramadan Goal

_____
_____
_____
_____
_____

Quran Study

before		after
start: surah .... ayah .... finish: surah .... ayah	**FAJR**	start: surah .... ayah .... finish: surah .... ayah ....
start: surah .... ayah .... finish: surah .... ayah	**DHUHR**	start: surah .... ayah .... finish: surah .... ayah ....
start: surah .... ayah .... finish: surah .... ayah	**ASR**	start: surah .... ayah .... finish: surah .... ayah ....
start: surah .... ayah .... finish: surah .... ayah	**MAGHRIB**	start: surah .... ayah .... finish: surah .... ayah ....
start: surah .... ayah .... finish: surah .... ayah	**ISHA'A**	start: surah .... ayah .... finish: surah .... ayah ....

Reflection

_____

_____

_____

_____

_____

_____

_____

Applecation

_____

_____

_____

_____

_____

To Do List

- [ ] _____
- [ ] _____
- [ ] _____
- [ ] _____
- [ ] _____
- [ ] _____
- [ ] _____
- [ ] _____

Meal Planner

SAHUR	IFTAR	DINNER

Water Tracker

Adequate Daily Fluid Intake is:

15.5 cups (3.7 liters) a day for men

11.5 cups (2.7 liters) a day for women

Date _____

Ramadan Day 7

Mood

○ HAPPY   ○ OKAY

○ INSPIRED   ○ TIRED

○ PEACEFUL   ○ ANGRY

Du'a of the Day

رَبَّنَا ٱغْفِرْ لَنَا ذُنُوبَنَا وَ إِسْرَافَنَا فِى أَمْرِنَا وَ ثَبِّتْ أَقْدَامَنَا وَ ٱنصُرْنَا عَلَى ٱلْقَوْمِ ٱلْكَـٰفِرِينَ

(آل عمران: 147)

Rabbanā igh'fir Lanā Dhunūbanā Wa-is'rāfanā
Fī Amrinā Wathabbit Aqdāmanā Wa-unşur'nā
`Alá L-Qawmi L-Kāfirīna

(Ali'imran :147)

Our Lord! Forgive our sins and excesses,
make our steps firm, and grant us victory
over the disbelieving people.

Reflection _____

_____

_____

_____

_____

_____

_____

Salah Tracker

FAJR
| S 2 | F 2 |

DHUHR
| S 4 | F 4 | S 2 | N 2 |

ASR
| S 4 | F 4 |

MAGHRIB
| F 3 | S 2 | N 2 |

ISHA'A
| S 4 | F 4 | S 2 | N 2 | W 3 | N 2 |

TARAWIH
| S 2 | S 2 | S 2 | S 2 | S 2 | S 2 | S 2 | S 2 |

Today's Deeds

○ QURAN

○ DUAS

○ KIND ACTION

_____

_____

_____

○ SADAQA

○ GOOD SPEECH

○ NIGHT PRAYER

_____

_____

_____

Tomorrow's Ramadan Goal

_____
_____
_____
_____
_____

Quran Study

before		after
start: surah .... ayah .... finish: surah .... ayah	**FAJR**	start: surah .... ayah .... finish: surah .... ayah ....
start: surah .... ayah .... finish: surah .... ayah	**DHUHR**	start: surah .... ayah .... finish: surah .... ayah ....
start: surah .... ayah .... finish: surah .... ayah	**ASR**	start: surah .... ayah .... finish: surah .... ayah ....
start: surah .... ayah .... finish: surah .... ayah	**MAGHRIB**	start: surah .... ayah .... finish: surah .... ayah ....
start: surah .... ayah .... finish: surah .... ayah	**ISHA'A**	start: surah .... ayah .... finish: surah .... ayah ....

Reflection

_____
_____
_____
_____
_____
_____
_____
_____
_____
_____

Applecation

_____
_____
_____
_____
_____
_____

To Do List

- [ ] _____
- [ ] _____
- [ ] _____
- [ ] _____
- [ ] _____
- [ ] _____
- [ ] _____
- [ ] _____

Meal Planner

SAHUR	IFTAR	DINNER

Water Tracker

Adequate Daily Fluid Intake is:

15.5 cups (3.7 liters) a day for men

11.5 cups (2.7 liters) a day for women

Date _____

Ramadan Day 8

Mood

○ HAPPY   ○ OKAY

○ INSPIRED   ○ TIRED

○ PEACEFUL   ○ ANGRY

Du'a of the Day

رَبَّنَا ظَلَمْنَا أَنفُسَنَا وَإِن لَّمْ تَغْفِرْ لَنَا وَتَرْحَمْنَا لَنَكُونَنَّ

مِنَ ٱلْخَٰسِرِينَ

(الأَعْرَاف: 23)

**Rabbanā Žalamnā Anfusanā
Wa-in Lam Taghfir Lanā WaTarĥamnā
Lanakūnanna Mina L-Khāsirīna**

(Al-araf:23)

Our Lord! We have wronged ourselves.
If You do not forgive us and have mercy on us,
we will certainly be losers.

Reflection _____

_____

_____

_____

_____

_____

Salah Tracker

FAJR
- S 2
- F 2

DHUHR
- S 4
- F 4
- S 2
- N 2

ASR
- S 4
- F 4

MAGHRIB
- F 3
- S 2
- N 2

ISHA'A
- S 4
- F 4
- S 2
- N 2
- W 3
- N 2

TARAWIH
- S 2
- S 2
- S 2
- S 2
- S 2
- S 2
- S 2
- S 2

Today's Deeds

○ QURAN

○ DUAS

○ KIND ACTION

_____

_____

_____

○ SADAQA

○ GOOD SPEECH

○ NIGHT PRAYER

_____

_____

_____

Tomorrow's Ramadan Goal

_____
_____
_____
_____
_____

Quran Study

before		after
start: surah .... ayah .... finish: surah .... ayah	**FAJR**	start: surah .... ayah .... finish: surah .... ayah ....
start: surah .... ayah .... finish: surah .... ayah	**DHUHR**	start: surah .... ayah .... finish: surah .... ayah ....
start: surah .... ayah .... finish: surah .... ayah	**ASR**	start: surah .... ayah .... finish: surah .... ayah ....
start: surah .... ayah .... finish: surah .... ayah	**MAGHRIB**	start: surah .... ayah .... finish: surah .... ayah ....
start: surah .... ayah .... finish: surah .... ayah	**ISHA'A**	start: surah .... ayah .... finish: surah .... ayah ....

Reflection

_____
_____
_____
_____
_____
_____
_____
_____
_____

Applecation

_____
_____
_____
_____
_____
_____

To Do List

- ☐ _____
- ☐ _____
- ☐ _____
- ☐ _____
- ☐ _____
- ☐ _____
- ☐ _____
- ☐ _____

Meal Planner

SAHUR	IFTAR	DINNER

Water Tracker

Adequate Daily Fluid Intake is:

15.5 cups (3.7 liters) a day for men

11.5 cups (2.7 liters) a day for women

Date _____

Ramadan Day 9

Mood

○ HAPPY   ○ OKAY
○ INSPIRED   ○ TIRED
○ PEACEFUL   ○ ANGRY

Du'a of the Day

رَبَّنَا لَا تَجْعَلْنَا مَعَ ٱلْقَوْمِ ٱلظَّـٰلِمِينَ

(الأعْرَاف: 47)

Rabbanā Lā Taj`alnā Ma`a l-qawmi L-žālimīna

(Al-araf:47)

Our Lord! Do not join us with the wrongdoing people

Reflection _____

_____

_____

_____

_____

_____

Salah Tracker

FAJR
S 2 F 2

DHUHR
S 4 F 4 S 2 N 2

ASR
S 4 F 4

MAGHRIB
F 3 S 2 N 2

ISHA'A
S 4 F 4 S 2 N 2 W 3 N 2

TARAWIH
S 2 S 2 S 2 S 2 S 2 S 2 S 2 S 2

Today's Deeds

○ QURAN
_____
_____

○ DUAS
_____
_____

○ KIND ACTION
_____
_____

○ SADAQA
_____
_____

○ GOOD SPEECH
_____
_____

○ NIGHT PRAYER
_____
_____

Tomorrow's Ramadan Goal

_____
_____
_____
_____
_____

Quran Study

before		after
start: surah .... ayah .... finish: surah .... ayah	**FAJR**	start: surah .... ayah .... finish: surah .... ayah ....
start: surah .... ayah .... finish: surah .... ayah	**DHUHR**	start: surah .... ayah .... finish: surah .... ayah ....
start: surah .... ayah .... finish: surah .... ayah	**ASR**	start: surah .... ayah .... finish: surah .... ayah ....
start: surah .... ayah .... finish: surah .... ayah	**MAGHRIB**	start: surah .... ayah .... finish: surah .... ayah ....
start: surah .... ayah .... finish: surah .... ayah	**ISHA'A**	start: surah .... ayah .... finish: surah .... ayah ....

Reflection

_____

_____

_____

_____

_____

_____

_____

Application

_____

_____

_____

_____

_____

To Do List

- [ ] _____
- [ ] _____
- [ ] _____
- [ ] _____
- [ ] _____
- [ ] _____
- [ ] _____
- [ ] _____

Meal Planner

SAHUR	IFTAR	DINNER

Water Tracker

Adequate Daily Fluid Intake is:
   15.5 cups (3.7 liters) a day for men
   11.5 cups (2.7 liters) a day for women

Date _____

Ramadan Day 10

Mood

○ HAPPY   ○ OKAY

○ INSPIRED   ○ TIRED

○ PEACEFUL   ○ ANGRY

Du'a of the Day

رَبَّنَا اَفْتَحْ بَيْنَنَا وَبَيْنَ قَوْمِنَا بِالْحَقِّ وَأَنتَ خَيْرُ الْفَـٰتِحِينَ

(الْأَعْرَاف: 89)

Rabbanā Af'taĥ Baynanā Wabayna Qawminā Bil-Ĥaqqi Wa-Anta Khayru L-fātiĥīna

(Al-araf:89)

Our Lord! Judge between us and our people with truth. You are the best of those who judge.

Reflection _____

_____

_____

_____

_____

_____

_____

Salah Tracker

FAJR
S 2 · **F 2**

DHUHR
S 4 · **F 4** · **S 2** · **N 2**

ASR
S 4 · **F 4**

MAGHRIB
F 3 · **S 2** · **N 2**

ISHA'A
S 4 · **F 4** · **S 2** · **N 2** · **W 3** · **N 2**

TARAWIH
S 2 · **S 2** · **S 2** · **S 2** · **S 2** · **S 2** · **S 2** · **S 2**

Today's Deeds

○ QURAN

_____

○ DUAS

_____

○ KIND ACTION

_____

○ SADAQA

_____

○ GOOD SPEECH

_____

○ NIGHT PRAYER

_____

Tomorrow's Ramadan Goal

_____

_____

_____

_____

_____

Quran Study

before		after
start: surah .... ayah .... finish: surah .... ayah	**FAJR**	start: surah .... ayah .... finish: surah .... ayah ....
start: surah .... ayah .... finish: surah .... ayah	**DHUHR**	start: surah .... ayah .... finish: surah .... ayah ....
start: surah .... ayah .... finish: surah .... ayah	**ASR**	start: surah .... ayah .... finish: surah .... ayah ....
start: surah .... ayah .... finish: surah .... ayah	**MAGHRIB**	start: surah .... ayah .... finish: surah .... ayah ....
start: surah .... ayah .... finish: surah .... ayah	**ISHA'A**	start: surah .... ayah .... finish: surah .... ayah ....

Reflection

_____

_____

_____

_____

_____

_____

_____

_____

_____

_____

Applecation

_____

_____

_____

_____

_____

_____

To Do List

- [ ]
- [ ]
- [ ]
- [ ]
- [ ]
- [ ]
- [ ]
- [ ]

Meal Planner

SAHUR	IFTAR	DINNER

Water Tracker

Adequate Daily Fluid Intake is:

15.5 cups (3.7 liters) a day for men

11.5 cups (2.7 liters) a day for women

Ramadan Day 11

Mood

○ HAPPY   ○ OKAY
○ INSPIRED ○ TIRED
○ PEACEFUL ○ ANGRY

Du'a of the Day

رَبَّنَآ أَفْرِغْ عَلَيْنَا صَبْرًا وَتَوَفَّنَا مُسْلِمِينَ

(الأَعْرَاف:126)

**Rabbanā Afrigh `Alaynā Şabran
Watawaffanā Mus'limīna**

(Al–araf:126)

Our Lord! Shower us with perseverance,
and let us die while submitting ʾto Youʾ.

Reflection _____

_____
_____
_____
_____
_____
_____

Salah Tracker

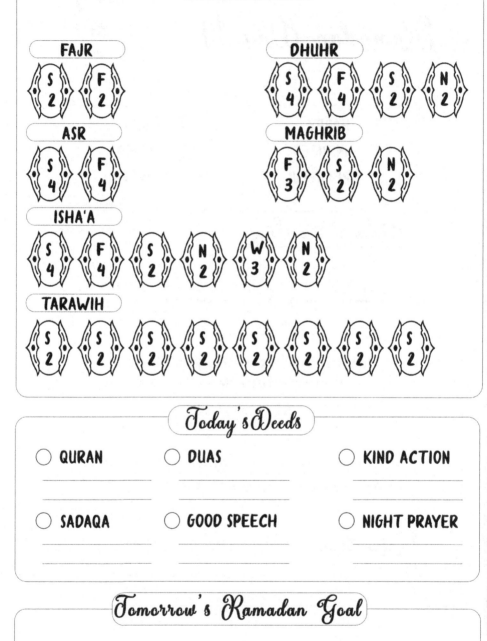

FAJR
- S 2
- F 2

DHUHR
- S 4
- F 4
- S 2
- N 2

ASR
- S 4
- F 4

MAGHRIB
- F 3
- S 2
- N 2

ISHA'A
- S 4
- F 4
- S 2
- N 2
- W 3
- N 2

TARAWIH
- S 2
- S 2
- S 2
- S 2
- S 2
- S 2
- S 2
- S 2

Today's Deeds

- ○ QURAN
- ○ DUAS
- ○ KIND ACTION
- ○ SADAQA
- ○ GOOD SPEECH
- ○ NIGHT PRAYER

Tomorrow's Ramadan Goal

Quran Study

before		after
start: surah .... ayah .... finish: surah .... ayah	**FAJR**	start: surah .... ayah .... finish: surah .... ayah ....
start: surah .... ayah .... finish: surah .... ayah	**DHUHR**	start: surah .... ayah .... finish: surah .... ayah ....
start: surah .... ayah .... finish: surah .... ayah	**ASR**	start: surah .... ayah .... finish: surah .... ayah ....
start: surah .... ayah .... finish: surah .... ayah	**MAGHRIB**	start: surah .... ayah .... finish: surah .... ayah ....
start: surah .... ayah .... finish: surah .... ayah	**ISHA'A**	start: surah .... ayah .... finish: surah .... ayah ....

Reflection

_____
_____
_____
_____
_____
_____
_____
_____

Applecation

_____
_____
_____
_____
_____
_____

To Do List

- ☐ _____
- ☐ _____
- ☐ _____
- ☐ _____

- ☐ _____
- ☐ _____
- ☐ _____
- ☐ _____

Meal Planner

SAHUR	IFTAR	DINNER

Water Tracker

Adequate Daily Fluid Intake is:

15.5 cups (3.7 liters) a day for men

11.5 cups (2.7 liters) a day for women

Date _____

Ramadan Day 12

Mood

○ HAPPY   ○ OKAY
○ INSPIRED ○ TIRED
○ PEACEFUL ○ ANGRY

Du'a of the Day

فَقَالُوا۟ عَلَى ٱللَّهِ تَوَكَّلْنَا رَبَّنَا لَا تَجْعَلْنَا فِتْنَةً لِّلْقَوْمِ
ٱلظَّٰلِمِينَ

(يُونس: 85)

Faqālū `Alá L-lahi Tawakkalnā Rabbanā
Lā Taj`alnā Fit'natan Lil'qawmi L-ẓālimīna

(Yunus:85)

They replied, "In Allah we trust. Our Lord! Do not
subject us to the persecution of
the oppressive people

Reflection _____

_____

_____

_____

_____

_____

_____

Salah Tracker

FAJR
- S 2
- F 2

DHUHR
- S 4
- F 4
- S 2
- N 2

ASR
- S 4
- F 4

MAGHRIB
- F 3
- S 2
- N 2

ISHA'A
- S 4
- F 4
- S 2
- N 2
- W 3
- N 2

TARAWIH
- S 2
- S 2
- S 2
- S 2
- S 2
- S 2
- S 2
- S 2

Today's Deeds

○ QURAN

○ DUAS

○ KIND ACTION

○ SADAQA

○ GOOD SPEECH

○ NIGHT PRAYER

Tomorrow's Ramadan Goal

Quran Study

before		after
start: surah .... ayah .... finish: surah .... ayah	**FAJR**	start: surah .... ayah .... finish: surah .... ayah ....
start: surah .... ayah .... finish: surah .... ayah	**DHUHR**	start: surah .... ayah .... finish: surah .... ayah ....
start: surah .... ayah .... finish: surah .... ayah	**ASR**	start: surah .... ayah .... finish: surah .... ayah ....
start: surah .... ayah .... finish: surah .... ayah	**MAGHRIB**	start: surah .... ayah .... finish: surah .... ayah ....
start: surah .... ayah .... finish: surah .... ayah	**ISHA'A**	start: surah .... ayah .... finish: surah .... ayah ....

Reflection

_____
_____
_____
_____
_____
_____
_____

Applecation

_____
_____
_____
_____
_____

To Do List

- ☐ _____
- ☐ _____
- ☐ _____
- ☐ _____
- ☐ _____
- ☐ _____
- ☐ _____
- ☐ _____

Meal Planner

SAHUR	IFTAR	DINNER

Water Tracker

Adequate Daily Fluid Intake is:

15.5 cups (3.7 liters) a day for men

11.5 cups (2.7 liters) a day for women

Date _____

Ramadan Day 13

Mood

- ○ HAPPY
- ○ INSPIRED
- ○ PEACEFUL
- ○ OKAY
- ○ TIRED
- ○ ANGRY

Du'a of the Day

قَالَ رَبِّ إِنِّى أَعُوذُ بِكَ أَنْ أَسْئَلَكَ مَا لَيْسَ لِى بِهِۦ عِلْمٌ وَإِلَّا تَغْفِرْ لِى وَتَرْحَمْنِىٓ أَكُن مِّنَ ٱلْخَٰسِرِينَ

(هود: 47)

Qāla Rabbi Innī A'ūdhu Bika An As'alaka
Mā Laysa Lī Bihi `il'mun Wa-illā Taghfir Lī
Watarhamnī Akun Mina L-khāsirīna
(Hud: 47)

Noah pleaded, My Lord, I seek refuge in You from
asking You about what I have no knowledge of,
and unless You forgive me and have
mercy on me, I will be one of the losers.

Reflection _____

_____

_____

_____

_____

_____

_____

Salah Tracker

FAJR
(S 2) (F 2)

DHUHR
(S 4) (F 4) (S 2) (N 2)

ASR
(S 4) (F 4)

MAGHRIB
(F 3) (S 2) (N 2)

ISHA'A
(S 4) (F 4) (S 2) (N 2) (W 3) (N 2)

TARAWIH
(S 2) (S 2) (S 2) (S 2) (S 2) (S 2) (S 2) (S 2)

Today's Deeds

○ QURAN
_____
_____

○ DUAS
_____
_____

○ KIND ACTION
_____
_____

○ SADAQA
_____
_____

○ GOOD SPEECH
_____
_____

○ NIGHT PRAYER
_____
_____

Tomorrow's Ramadan Goal

_____
_____
_____
_____
_____

Quran Study

before		after
start: surah .... ayah .... finish: surah .... ayah	**FAJR**	start: surah .... ayah .... finish: surah .... ayah ....
start: surah .... ayah .... finish: surah .... ayah	**DHUHR**	start: surah .... ayah .... finish: surah .... ayah ....
start: surah .... ayah .... finish: surah .... ayah	**ASR**	start: surah .... ayah .... finish: surah .... ayah ....
start: surah .... ayah .... finish: surah .... ayah	**MAGHRIB**	start: surah .... ayah .... finish: surah .... ayah ....
start: surah .... ayah .... finish: surah .... ayah	**ISHA'A**	start: surah .... ayah .... finish: surah .... ayah ....

Reflection

_____

_____

_____

_____

_____

_____

_____

_____

_____

Applecation

_____

_____

_____

_____

_____

_____

To Do List

- [ ] _____
- [ ] _____
- [ ] _____
- [ ] _____
- [ ] _____
- [ ] _____
- [ ] _____
- [ ] _____

Meal Planner

SAHUR	IFTAR	DINNER

Water Tracker

Adequate Daily Fluid Intake is:

15.5 cups (3.7 liters) a day for men
11.5 cups (2.7 liters) a day for women

Date _____

Ramadan Day 14

Mood

○ HAPPY   ○ OKAY

○ INSPIRED   ○ TIRED

○ PEACEFUL   ○ ANGRY

Du'a of the Day

رَبَّنَآ إِنَّكَ تَعْلَمُ مَا نُخْفِى وَمَا نُعْلِنُ وَمَا يَخْفَىٰ عَلَى ٱللَّهِ مِن شَىْءٍ فِى ٱلْأَرْضِ وَلَا فِى ٱلسَّمَآءِ

(إِبْرَاهِيمِ: 38)

Rabbanā innaka Ta`lamu Mā Nukh'fī
Wamā Nu``linu Wamā Yakhfá `Alá L-lahi
Min Shay'in Fī L-arđi Walā Fī L-samāi

('Ibrahim: 38)

Our Lord! You certainly know what we conceal
and what we reveal. Nothing on earth
or in heaven is hidden from Allah.

Reflection _____

_____

_____

_____

_____

_____

_____

Salah Tracker

FAJR
S 2 · **F 2**

DHUHR
S 4 · **F 4** · **S 2** · **N 2**

ASR
S 4 · **F 4**

MAGHRIB
F 3 · **S 2** · **N 2**

ISHA'A
S 4 · **F 4** · **S 2** · **N 2** · **W 3** · **N 2**

TARAWIH
S 2 · **S 2** · **S 2** · **S 2** · **S 2** · **S 2** · **S 2** · **S 2**

Today's Deeds

○ QURAN

○ DUAS

○ KIND ACTION

_____

_____

_____

○ SADAQA

○ GOOD SPEECH

○ NIGHT PRAYER

_____

_____

_____

Tomorrow's Ramadan Goal

_____
_____
_____
_____
_____

Quran Study

before		after
start: surah .... ayah .... finish: surah .... ayah	**FAJR**	start: surah .... ayah .... finish: surah .... ayah ....
start: surah .... ayah .... finish: surah .... ayah	**DHUHR**	start: surah .... ayah .... finish: surah .... ayah ....
start: surah .... ayah .... finish: surah .... ayah	**ASR**	start: surah .... ayah .... finish: surah .... ayah ....
start: surah .... ayah .... finish: surah .... ayah	**MAGHRIB**	start: surah .... ayah .... finish: surah .... ayah ....
start: surah .... ayah .... finish: surah .... ayah	**ISHA'A**	start: surah .... ayah .... finish: surah .... ayah ....

Reflection

_____
_____
_____
_____
_____
_____
_____
_____

Applecation

_____
_____
_____
_____
_____

To Do List

- [ ] _____
- [ ] _____
- [ ] _____
- [ ] _____
- [ ] _____
- [ ] _____
- [ ] _____
- [ ] _____

Meal Planner

SAHUR	IFTAR	DINNER

Water Tracker

Adequate Daily Fluid Intake is:

15.5 cups (3.7 liters) a day for men

11.5 cups (2.7 liters) a day for women

Ramadan Day 15

Mood

○ HAPPY   ○ OKAY

○ INSPIRED   ○ TIRED

○ PEACEFUL   ○ ANGRY

Du'a of the Day

رَبِّ ٱجْعَلْنِى مُقِيمَ ٱلصَّلَوٰةِ وَمِن ذُرِّيَّتِى رَبَّنَا وَتَقَبَّلْ دُعَآءِ
(إِبْرَاهِيم: 40)

Rabbi ij''alnī Muqīma L-ṣalati Wamin Dhurriyyatī ͏ Rabbanā Wataqabbal Du`āi

('Ibrahim: 40)

My Lord! Make me and those ʿbelieversʾ of my descendants keep up prayer. Our Lord! Accept my prayers.

Reflection _____

_____

_____

_____

_____

_____

_____

Salah Tracker

FAJR
S 2 | F 2

DHUHR
S 4 | F 4 | S 2 | N 2

ASR
S 4 | F 4

MAGHRIB
F 3 | S 2 | N 2

ISHA'A
S 4 | F 4 | S 2 | N 2 | W 3 | N 2

TARAWIH
S 2 | S 2 | S 2 | S 2 | S 2 | S 2 | S 2 | S 2

Today's Deeds

○ QURAN   ○ DUAS   ○ KIND ACTION
_____   _____   _____

○ SADAQA   ○ GOOD SPEECH   ○ NIGHT PRAYER
_____   _____   _____

Tomorrow's Ramadan Goal
_____
_____
_____
_____
_____

Quran Study

before		after
start: surah .... ayah .... finish: surah .... ayah	**FAJR**	start: surah .... ayah .... finish: surah .... ayah ....
start: surah .... ayah .... finish: surah .... ayah	**DHUHR**	start: surah .... ayah .... finish: surah .... ayah ....
start: surah .... ayah .... finish: surah .... ayah	**ASR**	start: surah .... ayah .... finish: surah .... ayah ....
start: surah .... ayah .... finish: surah .... ayah	**MAGHRIB**	start: surah .... ayah .... finish: surah .... ayah ....
start: surah .... ayah .... finish: surah .... ayah	**ISHA'A**	start: surah .... ayah .... finish: surah .... ayah ....

Reflection

_____
_____
_____
_____
_____
_____
_____

Applecation

_____
_____
_____
_____
_____

To Do List

- [ ] _____
- [ ] _____
- [ ] _____
- [ ] _____
- [ ] _____
- [ ] _____
- [ ] _____
- [ ] _____

Meal Planner

SAHUR	IFTAR	DINNER

Water Tracker

Adequate Daily Fluid Intake is:

15.5 cups (3.7 liters) a day for men

11.5 cups (2.7 liters) a day for women

Date _____

Ramadan Day 16

Mood

○ HAPPY   ○ OKAY

○ INSPIRED   ○ TIRED

○ PEACEFUL   ○ ANGRY

Du'a of the Day

رَبَّنَا ٱغۡفِرۡ لِي وَلِوَٰلِدَيَّ وَلِلۡمُؤۡمِنِينَ يَوۡمَ يَقُومُ ٱلۡحِسَابُ

(إِبۡرَاهِيم: 41)

**Rabbanā igh'fir Lī Waliwālidayya
Walil'mu'uminīna Yawma Yaqūmu l-Ĥisābu**

('Ibrahim: 41)

Our Lord! Forgive me, my parents,
and the believers on the Day when
the judgment will come to pass

Reflection _____

_____

_____

_____

_____

_____

Salah Tracker

FAJR
S 2 | F 2

DHUHR
S 4 | F 4 | S 2 | N 2

ASR
S 4 | F 4

MAGHRIB
F 3 | S 2 | N 2

ISHA'A
S 4 | F 4 | S 2 | N 2 | W 3 | N 2

TARAWIH
S 2 | S 2 | S 2 | S 2 | S 2 | S 2 | S 2 | S 2

Today's Deeds

○ QURAN
_____
_____

○ DUAS
_____
_____

○ KIND ACTION
_____
_____

○ SADAQA
_____
_____

○ GOOD SPEECH
_____
_____

○ NIGHT PRAYER
_____
_____

Tomorrow's Ramadan Goal

_____
_____
_____
_____
_____

Quran Study

before		after
start: surah .... ayah .... finish: surah .... ayah	**FAJR**	start: surah .... ayah .... finish: surah .... ayah ....
start: surah .... ayah .... finish: surah .... ayah	**DHUHR**	start: surah .... ayah .... finish: surah .... ayah ....
start: surah .... ayah .... finish: surah .... ayah	**ASR**	start: surah .... ayah .... finish: surah .... ayah ....
start: surah .... ayah .... finish: surah .... ayah	**MAGHRIB**	start: surah .... ayah .... finish: surah .... ayah ....
start: surah .... ayah .... finish: surah .... ayah	**ISHA'A**	start: surah .... ayah .... finish: surah .... ayah ....

Reflection

_____
_____
_____
_____
_____
_____
_____
_____
_____

Applecation

_____
_____
_____
_____
_____

To Do List

- [ ] _____
- [ ] _____
- [ ] _____
- [ ] _____
- [ ] _____
- [ ] _____
- [ ] _____
- [ ] _____

Meal Planner

SAHUR	IFTAR	DINNER

Water Tracker

Adequate Daily Fluid Intake is:

15.5 cups (3.7 liters) a day for men

11.5 cups (2.7 liters) a day for women

Date _____

Ramadan Day 17

Mood

○ HAPPY   ○ OKAY

○ INSPIRED   ○ TIRED

○ PEACEFUL   ○ ANGRY

Du'a of the Day

وَقُل رَّبِّ أَدْخِلْنِى مُدْخَلَ صِدْقٍ وَأَخْرِجْنِى مُخْرَجَ صِدْقٍ وَاجْعَل لِّى مِن لَّدُنكَ سُلْطَـٰنًا نَّصِيرًا

(الإسراء:80)

Waqul Rabbi adkhil'nī Mud'khala Şid'qin Wa-akhrij'nī Mukh'raja Şid'qin Wa-ij'`al Lī Min Ladunka Sul'ţānan Naşīran

⟨Al-Isra: 80⟩

And say, "My Lord! Grant me an honourable entrance and an honourable exit and give me a supporting authority from Yourself."

Reflection _____

_____

_____

_____

_____

_____

_____

Salah Tracker

FAJR

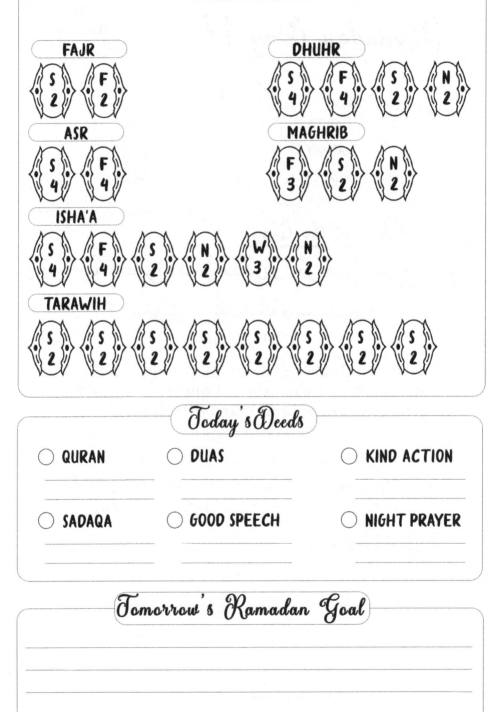

S 2 — F 2

DHUHR

S 4 — F 4 — S 2 — N 2

ASR

S 4 — F 4

MAGHRIB

F 3 — S 2 — N 2

ISHA'A

S 4 — F 4 — S 2 — N 2 — W 3 — N 2

TARAWIH

S 2 — S 2 — S 2 — S 2 — S 2 — S 2 — S 2 — S 2

Today's Deeds

○ QURAN

○ DUAS

○ KIND ACTION

○ SADAQA

○ GOOD SPEECH

○ NIGHT PRAYER

Tomorrow's Ramadan Goal

Quran Study

before		after
start: surah .... ayah .... finish: surah .... ayah	**FAJR**	start: surah .... ayah .... finish: surah .... ayah ....
start: surah .... ayah .... finish: surah .... ayah	**DHUHR**	start: surah .... ayah .... finish: surah .... ayah ....
start: surah .... ayah .... finish: surah .... ayah	**ASR**	start: surah .... ayah .... finish: surah .... ayah ....
start: surah .... ayah .... finish: surah .... ayah	**MAGHRIB**	start: surah .... ayah .... finish: surah .... ayah ....
start: surah .... ayah .... finish: surah .... ayah	**ISHA'A**	start: surah .... ayah .... finish: surah .... ayah ....

Reflection

_____

_____

_____

_____

_____

_____

_____

_____

_____

Application

_____

_____

_____

_____

_____

_____

To Do List

- ☐ ────────────────
- ☐ ────────────────
- ☐ ────────────────
- ☐ ────────────────

- ☐ ────────────────
- ☐ ────────────────
- ☐ ────────────────
- ☐ ────────────────

Meal Planner

SAHUR	IFTAR	DINNER

Water Tracker

Adequate Daily Fluid Intake is:

15.5 cups (3.7 liters) a day for men

11.5 cups (2.7 liters) a day for women

Ramadan Day 18

Mood

○ HAPPY   ○ OKAY

○ INSPIRED   ○ TIRED

○ PEACEFUL   ○ ANGRY

Du'a of the Day

رَبَّنَآ ءَاتِنَا مِن لَّدُنكَ رَحْمَةً وَهَيِّئْ لَنَا مِنْ أَمْرِنَا رَشَدًا

(الكهف: 10)

**Rabbanā ātinā min ladunka raĥmatan wahayyi'
lanā min amrinā rashadan**

(Al-Kahf: 10)

Our Lord! Grant us mercy from Yourself
and guide us rightly through our ordeal.

Reflection _____

Salah Tracker

FAJR

S 2 | F 2

DHUHR

S 4 | F 4 | S 2 | N 2

ASR

S 4 | F 4

MAGHRIB

F 3 | S 2 | N 2

ISHA'A

S 4 | F 4 | S 2 | N 2 | W 3 | N 2

TARAWIH

S 2 | S 2 | S 2 | S 2 | S 2 | S 2 | S 2 | S 2

Today's Deeds

○ QURAN

_____
_____

○ SADAQA

_____
_____

○ DUAS

_____
_____

○ GOOD SPEECH

_____
_____

○ KIND ACTION

_____
_____

○ NIGHT PRAYER

_____
_____

Tomorrow's Ramadan Goal

_____
_____
_____
_____
_____

Quran Study

before		after
start: surah .... ayah .... finish: surah .... ayah	**FAJR**	start: surah .... ayah .... finish: surah .... ayah ....
start: surah .... ayah .... finish: surah .... ayah	**DHUHR**	start: surah .... ayah .... finish: surah .... ayah ....
start: surah .... ayah .... finish: surah .... ayah	**ASR**	start: surah .... ayah .... finish: surah .... ayah ....
start: surah .... ayah .... finish: surah .... ayah	**MAGHRIB**	start: surah .... ayah .... finish: surah .... ayah ....
start: surah .... ayah .... finish: surah .... ayah	**ISHA'A**	start: surah .... ayah .... finish: surah .... ayah ....

Reflection

_____
_____
_____
_____
_____
_____
_____

Application

_____
_____
_____
_____
_____

To Do List

- [ ]
- [ ]
- [ ]
- [ ]

- [ ]
- [ ]
- [ ]
- [ ]

Meal Planner

SAHUR	IFTAR	DINNER

Water Tracker

Adequate Daily Fluid Intake is:

15.5 cups (3.7 liters) a day for men
11.5 cups (2.7 liters) a day for women

Date _____

Ramadan Day 19

Mood

○ HAPPY   ○ OKAY
○ INSPIRED   ○ TIRED
○ PEACEFUL   ○ ANGRY

Du'a of the Day

قَالَ رَبِّ ٱشۡرَحۡ لِي صَدۡرِى ﴿٢٥﴾
وَيَسِّرۡ لِيٓ أَمۡرِى ﴿٢٦﴾
وَٱحۡلُلۡ عُقۡدَةً مِّن لِّسَانِي ﴿٢٧﴾
(طه)

Qāla Rabbi ish'raĥ lī şadrī ﴿25﴾
Wayassir lī amrī ﴿26﴾
Wa-uĥ'lul `uq'datan min lisānī ﴿27﴾
(Ta-Ha)

Moses prayed, My Lord! Uplift my heart for me,
and make my task easy,
and remove the impediment from my tongue

Reflection _____

Salah Tracker

FAJR
(S 2) (F 2)

DHUHR
(S 4) (F 4) (S 2) (N 2)

ASR
(S 4) (F 4)

MAGHRIB
(F 3) (S 2) (N 2)

ISHA'A
(S 4) (F 4) (S 2) (N 2) (W 3) (N 2)

TARAWIH
(S 2) (S 2) (S 2) (S 2) (S 2) (S 2) (S 2) (S 2)

Today's Deeds

○ QURAN ○ DUAS ○ KIND ACTION
_____ _____ _____
_____ _____ _____

○ SADAQA ○ GOOD SPEECH ○ NIGHT PRAYER
_____ _____ _____
_____ _____ _____

Tomorrow's Ramadan Goal

_____
_____
_____
_____
_____

Quran Study

before		after
start: surah .... ayah .... finish: surah .... ayah	**FAJR**	start: surah .... ayah .... finish: surah .... ayah ....
start: surah .... ayah .... finish: surah .... ayah	**DHUHR**	start: surah .... ayah .... finish: surah .... ayah ....
start: surah .... ayah .... finish: surah .... ayah	**ASR**	start: surah .... ayah .... finish: surah .... ayah ....
start: surah .... ayah .... finish: surah .... ayah	**MAGHRIB**	start: surah .... ayah .... finish: surah .... ayah ....
start: surah .... ayah .... finish: surah .... ayah	**ISHA'A**	start: surah .... ayah .... finish: surah .... ayah ....

Reflection

_____

_____

_____

_____

_____

_____

_____

_____

_____

Applecation

_____

_____

_____

_____

_____

_____

To Do List

- [ ]
- [ ]
- [ ]
- [ ]
- [ ]
- [ ]
- [ ]
- [ ]

Meal Planner

SAHUR	IFTAR	DINNER

Water Tracker

Adequate Daily Fluid Intake is:

15.5 cups (3.7 liters) a day for men

11.5 cups (2.7 liters) a day for women

Date _____

Ramadan Day 20

Mood

- ○ HAPPY
- ○ INSPIRED
- ○ PEACEFUL
- ○ OKAY
- ○ TIRED
- ○ ANGRY

Du'a of the Day

رَّبِّ زِدْنِى عِلْمًا

(طه:114)

Rabbi zid'nī `il'man

(Ta-Ha:114)

My Lord! Increase me in knowledge.

Reflection

Salah Tracker

FAJR
S 2 · F 2

DHUHR
S 4 · F 4 · S 2 · N 2

ASR
S 4 · F 4

MAGHRIB
F 3 · S 2 · N 2

ISHA'A
S 4 · F 4 · S 2 · N 2 · W 3 · N 2

TARAWIH
S 2 · S 2 · S 2 · S 2 · S 2 · S 2 · S 2 · S 2

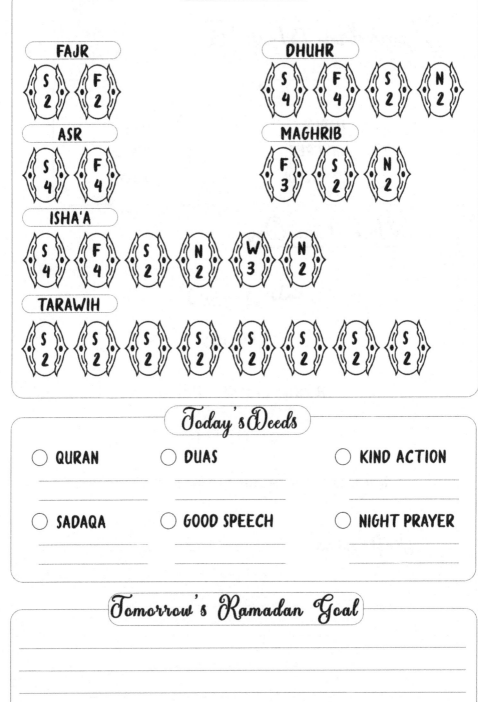

Today's Deeds

○ QURAN ○ DUAS ○ KIND ACTION
_____ _____ _____
_____ _____ _____

○ SADAQA ○ GOOD SPEECH ○ NIGHT PRAYER
_____ _____ _____
_____ _____ _____

Tomorrow's Ramadan Goal

_____
_____
_____
_____
_____

Quran Study

before		after
start: surah .... ayah .... finish: surah .... ayah	**FAJR**	start: surah .... ayah .... finish: surah .... ayah ....
start: surah .... ayah .... finish: surah .... ayah	**DHUHR**	start: surah .... ayah .... finish: surah .... ayah ....
start: surah .... ayah .... finish: surah .... ayah	**ASR**	start: surah .... ayah .... finish: surah .... ayah ....
start: surah .... ayah .... finish: surah .... ayah	**MAGHRIB**	start: surah .... ayah .... finish: surah .... ayah ....
start: surah .... ayah .... finish: surah .... ayah	**ISHA'A**	start: surah .... ayah .... finish: surah .... ayah ....

Reflection

_____
_____
_____
_____
_____
_____
_____
_____
_____

Applecation

_____
_____
_____
_____
_____

To Do List

- ☐ _____
- ☐ _____
- ☐ _____
- ☐ _____

- ☐ _____
- ☐ _____
- ☐ _____
- ☐ _____

Meal Planner

SAHUR	IFTAR	DINNER
_____	_____	_____
_____	_____	_____
_____	_____	_____
_____	_____	_____
_____	_____	_____
_____	_____	_____
_____	_____	_____
_____	_____	_____

Water Tracker

Adequate Daily Fluid Intake is:

15.5 cups (3.7 liters) a day for men

11.5 cups (2.7 liters) a day for women

Ramadan Day 21

Mood

○ HAPPY   ○ OKAY

○ INSPIRED   ○ TIRED

○ PEACEFUL   ○ ANGRY

Du'a of the Day

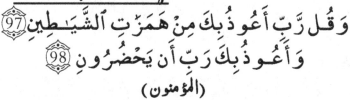

وَقُل رَّبِّ أَعُوذُ بِكَ مِنْ هَمَزَٰتِ ٱلشَّيَـٰطِينِ ۝

وَأَعُوذُ بِكَ رَبِّ أَن يَحْضُرُونِ ۝

(المؤمنون)

waqul Rabbi a`ūdhu bika min
hamazāti l-shayāṭīni ۝
Wa-a`ūdhu bika Rabbi an yaḥḍurūni ۝

(Al-Muminun)

And say, "My Lord! I seek refuge in You from
the temptations of the devils.*
And I seek refuge in You, my Lord,
that they ˹even˺ come near me."

Reflection _____

_____

_____

_____

_____

_____

Salah Tracker

FAJR
(S 2) (F 2)

DHUHR
(S 4) (F 4) (S 2) (N 2)

ASR
(S 4) (F 4)

MAGHRIB
(F 3) (S 2) (N 2)

ISHA'A
(S 4) (F 4) (S 2) (N 2) (W 3) (N 2)

TARAWIH
(S 2) (S 2) (S 2) (S 2) (S 2) (S 2) (S 2) (S 2)

Today's Deeds

○ QURAN _____

○ DUAS _____

○ KIND ACTION _____

○ SADAQA _____

○ GOOD SPEECH _____

○ NIGHT PRAYER _____

Tomorrow's Ramadan Goal

Quran Study

before		after
start: surah .... ayah .... finish: surah .... ayah	**FAJR**	start: surah .... ayah .... finish: surah .... ayah ....
start: surah .... ayah .... finish: surah .... ayah	**DHUHR**	start: surah .... ayah .... finish: surah .... ayah ....
start: surah .... ayah .... finish: surah .... ayah	**ASR**	start: surah .... ayah .... finish: surah .... ayah ....
start: surah .... ayah .... finish: surah .... ayah	**MAGHRIB**	start: surah .... ayah .... finish: surah .... ayah ....
start: surah .... ayah .... finish: surah .... ayah	**ISHA'A**	start: surah .... ayah .... finish: surah .... ayah ....

Reflection

_____
_____
_____
_____
_____
_____
_____
_____

Applecation

_____
_____
_____
_____
_____

To Do List

- ☐ _____ ☐ _____
- ☐ _____ ☐ _____
- ☐ _____ ☐ _____
- ☐ _____ ☐ _____

Meal Planner

SAHUR	IFTAR	DINNER
_____	_____	_____
_____	_____	_____
_____	_____	_____
_____	_____	_____
_____	_____	_____
_____	_____	_____
_____	_____	_____
_____	_____	_____

Water Tracker

Adequate Daily Fluid Intake is:

15.5 cups (3.7 liters) a day for men

11.5 cups (2.7 liters) a day for women

Date _____

Ramadan Day 22

Mood

○ HAPPY   ○ OKAY

○ INSPIRED   ○ TIRED

○ PEACEFUL   ○ ANGRY

Du'a of the Day

رَبَّنَآ ءَامَنَّا فَٱغْفِرْ لَنَا وَٱرْحَمْنَا وَأَنتَ خَيْرُ ٱلرَّٰحِمِينَ

[المؤمنون: 109]

**Rabbanā āmannā fa-igh'fir lanā
wa-ir'ĥamnā wa-anta khayru l-rāĥimīna**

(Al-Muminun: 109)

Our Lord! We have believed, so forgive us
and have mercy on us, for You are the best of those
who show mercy

Reflection _____

_____

_____

_____

_____

_____

_____

_____

Salah Tracker

FAJR
S 2 | F 2

DHUHR
S 4 | F 4 | S 2 | N 2

ASR
S 4 | F 4

MAGHRIB
F 3 | S 2 | N 2

ISHA'A
S 4 | F 4 | S 2 | N 2 | W 3 | N 2

TARAWIH
S 2 | S 2 | S 2 | S 2 | S 2 | S 2 | S 2 | S 2

Today's Deeds

○ QURAN
_____
_____

○ DUAS
_____
_____

○ KIND ACTION
_____
_____

○ SADAQA
_____
_____

○ GOOD SPEECH
_____
_____

○ NIGHT PRAYER
_____
_____

Tomorrow's Ramadan Goal

_____
_____
_____
_____
_____

Quran Study

before		after
start: surah .... ayah .... finish: surah .... ayah	**FAJR**	start: surah .... ayah .... finish: surah .... ayah ....
start: surah .... ayah .... finish: surah .... ayah	**DHUHR**	start: surah .... ayah .... finish: surah .... ayah ....
start: surah .... ayah .... finish: surah .... ayah	**ASR**	start: surah .... ayah .... finish: surah .... ayah ....
start: surah .... ayah .... finish: surah .... ayah	**MAGHRIB**	start: surah .... ayah .... finish: surah .... ayah ....
start: surah .... ayah .... finish: surah .... ayah	**ISHA'A**	start: surah .... ayah .... finish: surah .... ayah ....

Reflection

_____

_____

_____

_____

_____

_____

_____

_____

_____

Application

_____

_____

_____

_____

_____

To Do List

- [ ]
- [ ]
- [ ]
- [ ]
- [ ]
- [ ]
- [ ]
- [ ]

Meal Planner

SAHUR	IFTAR	DINNER

Water Tracker

Adequate Daily Fluid Intake is:

15.5 cups (3.7 liters) a day for men

11.5 cups (2.7 liters) a day for women

Date _____

Ramadan Day 23

Fasting

○ YES

○ NO

Mood

○ HAPPY   ○ OKAY

○ INSPIRED   ○ TIRED

○ PEACEFUL   ○ ANGRY

Du'a of the Day

رَّبِّ اغْفِرْ وَارْحَمْ وَأَنتَ خَيْرُ الرَّحِمِينَ

(المؤمنون: 118)

Rabbi igh'fir wa-ir'ham wa-anta khayru l-rāhimīna

(Al-Muminun: 118)

My Lord! Forgive and have mercy, for You are the best of those who show mercy.

Reflection _____

_____

_____

_____

_____

_____

Salah Tracker

FAJR
S 2 | F 2

DHUHR
S 4 | F 4 | S 2 | N 2

ASR
S 4 | F 4

MAGHRIB
F 3 | S 2 | N 2

ISHA'A
S 4 | F 4 | S 2 | N 2 | W 3 | N 2

TARAWIH
S 2 | S 2 | S 2 | S 2 | S 2 | S 2 | S 2 | S 2

Today's Deeds

○ QURAN

○ DUAS

○ KIND ACTION

○ SADAQA

○ GOOD SPEECH

○ NIGHT PRAYER

Tomorrow's Ramadan Goal

Quran Study

before		after
start: surah .... ayah .... finish: surah .... ayah	**FAJR**	start: surah .... ayah .... finish: surah .... ayah ....
start: surah .... ayah .... finish: surah .... ayah	**DHUHR**	start: surah .... ayah .... finish: surah .... ayah ....
start: surah .... ayah .... finish: surah .... ayah	**ASR**	start: surah .... ayah .... finish: surah .... ayah ....
start: surah .... ayah .... finish: surah .... ayah	**MAGHRIB**	start: surah .... ayah .... finish: surah .... ayah ....
start: surah .... ayah .... finish: surah .... ayah	**ISHA'A**	start: surah .... ayah .... finish: surah .... ayah ....

Reflection

Applecation

To Do List

- [ ] _____
- [ ] _____
- [ ] _____
- [ ] _____
- [ ] _____
- [ ] _____
- [ ] _____
- [ ] _____

Meal Planner

SAHUR	IFTAR	DINNER

Water Tracker

Adequate Daily Fluid Intake is:

15.5 cups (3.7 liters) a day for men

11.5 cups (2.7 liters) a day for women

Date _____

Ramadan Day 24

Mood

○ HAPPY   ○ OKAY
○ INSPIRED   ○ TIRED
○ PEACEFUL   ○ ANGRY

Du'a of the Day

رَبَّنَا اصْرِفْ عَنَّا عَذَابَ جَهَنَّمَ إِنَّ عَذَابَهَا كَانَ غَرَامًا ۝

إِنَّهَا سَاءَتْ مُسْتَقَرًّا وَمُقَامًا ۝

(الفرقان)

Rabbanā iş'rif `annā `adhāba Jahannama
inna `adhābahā kāna gharāman ⑥⑤
innahā sāat mus'taqarran wamuqāman ⑥⑥

(Al-Furqan: 65)

Our Lord! Keep the punishment of Hell away from us,
for its punishment is indeed unrelenting.
It is certainly an evil place to settle and reside.

Reflection _____

_____

_____

_____

_____

_____

_____

Salah Tracker

FAJR
S 2 | F 2

DHUHR
S 4 | F 4 | S 2 | N 2

ASR
S 4 | F 4

MAGHRIB
F 3 | S 2 | N 2

ISHA'A
S 4 | F 4 | S 2 | N 2 | W 3 | N 2

TARAWIH
S 2 | S 2 | S 2 | S 2 | S 2 | S 2 | S 2 | S 2

Today's Deeds

○ QURAN
_____
_____

○ DUAS
_____
_____

○ KIND ACTION
_____
_____

○ SADAQA
_____
_____

○ GOOD SPEECH
_____
_____

○ NIGHT PRAYER
_____
_____

Tomorrow's Ramadan Goal

_____
_____
_____
_____
_____

Quran Study

before		after
start: surah .... ayah .... finish: surah .... ayah	**FAJR**	start: surah .... ayah .... finish: surah .... ayah ....
start: surah .... ayah .... finish: surah .... ayah	**DHUHR**	start: surah .... ayah .... finish: surah .... ayah ....
start: surah .... ayah .... finish: surah .... ayah	**ASR**	start: surah .... ayah .... finish: surah .... ayah ....
start: surah .... ayah .... finish: surah .... ayah	**MAGHRIB**	start: surah .... ayah .... finish: surah .... ayah ....
start: surah .... ayah .... finish: surah .... ayah	**ISHA'A**	start: surah .... ayah .... finish: surah .... ayah ....

Reflection

_____
_____
_____
_____
_____
_____
_____

Applecation

_____
_____
_____
_____
_____

To Do List

- ☐ _____
- ☐ _____
- ☐ _____
- ☐ _____
- ☐ _____
- ☐ _____
- ☐ _____
- ☐ _____

Meal Planner

SAHUR	IFTAR	DINNER

Water Tracker

Adequate Daily Fluid Intake is:

15.5 cups (3.7 liters) a day for men

11.5 cups (2.7 liters) a day for women

Date _____

Ramadan Day 25

Mood

○ HAPPY   ○ OKAY
○ INSPIRED   ○ TIRED
○ PEACEFUL   ○ ANGRY

Du'a of the Day

رَبَّنَا هَبْ لَنَا مِنْ أَزْوَاجِنَا وَذُرِّيَّاتِنَا قُرَّةَ أَعْيُنٍ
وَاجْعَلْنَا لِلْمُتَّقِينَ إِمَامًا

[الفرقان: 74]

Rabbanā hab lanā min azwājinā wadhurriyyātinā qurrata a`yunin wa-ij``alnā lil'muttaqīna Imāman

(Al-Furqan: 74)

Our Lord! Bless us with ˹pious˺ spouses and offspring who will be the joy of our hearts, and make us models for the righteous.

Reflection _____

_____
_____
_____
_____
_____
_____

Salah Tracker

FAJR
S 2 | F 2

DHUHR
S 4 | F 4 | S 2 | N 2

ASR
S 4 | F 4

MAGHRIB
F 3 | S 2 | N 2

ISHA'A
S 4 | F 4 | S 2 | N 2 | W 3 | N 2

TARAWIH
S 2 | S 2 | S 2 | S 2 | S 2 | S 2 | S 2 | S 2

Today's Deeds

○ QURAN

○ DUAS

○ KIND ACTION

○ SADAQA

○ GOOD SPEECH

○ NIGHT PRAYER

Tomorrow's Ramadan Goal

Quran Study

before		after
start: surah .... ayah .... finish: surah .... ayah	**FAJR**	start: surah .... ayah .... finish: surah .... ayah ....
start: surah .... ayah .... finish: surah .... ayah	**DHUHR**	start: surah .... ayah .... finish: surah .... ayah ....
start: surah .... ayah .... finish: surah .... ayah	**ASR**	start: surah .... ayah .... finish: surah .... ayah ....
start: surah .... ayah .... finish: surah .... ayah	**MAGHRIB**	start: surah .... ayah .... finish: surah .... ayah ....
start: surah .... ayah .... finish: surah .... ayah	**ISHA'A**	start: surah .... ayah .... finish: surah .... ayah ....

Reflection

_____

_____

_____

_____

_____

_____

_____

_____

_____

Applecation

_____

_____

_____

_____

_____

_____

To Do List

- ☐ ──────────────
- ☐ ──────────────
- ☐ ──────────────
- ☐ ──────────────

- ☐ ──────────────
- ☐ ──────────────
- ☐ ──────────────
- ☐ ──────────────

Meal Planner

SAHUR	IFTAR	DINNER

Water Tracker

Adequate Daily Fluid Intake is:

15.5 cups (3.7 liters) a day for men

11.5 cups (2.7 liters) a day for women

Date _____

Ramadan Day 26

Mood

○ HAPPY   ○ OKAY

○ INSPIRED   ○ TIRED

○ PEACEFUL   ○ ANGRY

Du'a of the Day

رَبِّ إِنِّى ظَلَمْتُ نَفْسِى فَٱغْفِرْ لِى

(القصص: 16)

Rabbi innī žalamtu nafsī fa-igh'fir lī

(Al-Qasas:16)

My Lord! I have definitely wronged my soul,
so forgive me.

Reflection _____

Salah Tracker

FAJR
S 2 | F 2

DHUHR
S 4 | F 4 | S 2 | N 2

ASR
S 4 | F 4

MAGHRIB
F 3 | S 2 | N 2

ISHA'A
S 4 | F 4 | S 2 | N 2 | W 3 | N 2

TARAWIH
S 2 | S 2 | S 2 | S 2 | S 2 | S 2 | S 2 | S 2

Today's Deeds

○ QURAN   ○ DUAS   ○ KIND ACTION
_____   _____   _____
_____   _____   _____

○ SADAQA   ○ GOOD SPEECH   ○ NIGHT PRAYER
_____   _____   _____
_____   _____   _____

Tomorrow's Ramadan Goal

_____
_____
_____
_____
_____

Quran Study

before		after
start: surah .... ayah .... finish: surah .... ayah	**FAJR**	start: surah .... ayah .... finish: surah .... ayah ....
start: surah .... ayah .... finish: surah .... ayah	**DHUHR**	start: surah .... ayah .... finish: surah .... ayah ....
start: surah .... ayah .... finish: surah .... ayah	**ASR**	start: surah .... ayah .... finish: surah .... ayah ....
start: surah .... ayah .... finish: surah .... ayah	**MAGHRIB**	start: surah .... ayah .... finish: surah .... ayah ....
start: surah .... ayah .... finish: surah .... ayah	**ISHA'A**	start: surah .... ayah .... finish: surah .... ayah ....

Reflection

_____

_____
_____
_____
_____
_____
_____
_____
_____

Applecation

_____
_____
_____
_____
_____
_____

To Do List

- [ ] _____
- [ ] _____
- [ ] _____
- [ ] _____
- [ ] _____
- [ ] _____
- [ ] _____
- [ ] _____

Meal Planner

SAHUR	IFTAR	DINNER

Water Tracker

Adequate Daily Fluid Intake is:

15.5 cups (3.7 liters) a day for men

11.5 cups (2.7 liters) a day for women

Ramadan Day 27

Mood

○ HAPPY   ○ OKAY

○ INSPIRED   ○ TIRED

○ PEACEFUL   ○ ANGRY

Du'a of the Day

قَالَ رَبِّ بِمَآ أَنْعَمْتَ عَلَىَّ فَلَنْ أَكُونَ ظَهِيرًا لِّلْمُجْرِمِينَ

(القصص: 17)

Qāla Rabbi bimā an`amta `alayya falan akūna žahīran lil'muj'rimīna

(Al-Qasas:17)

Moses pledged, "My Lord! For all Your favours upon me, I will never side with the wicked."

Reflection _____

_____

_____

_____

_____

_____

_____

Salah Tracker

FAJR
S 2 | F 2

DHUHR
S 4 | F 4 | S 2 | N 2

ASR
S 4 | F 4

MAGHRIB
F 3 | S 2 | N 2

ISHA'A
S 4 | F 4 | S 2 | N 2 | W 3 | N 2

TARAWIH
S 2 | S 2 | S 2 | S 2 | S 2 | S 2 | S 2 | S 2

Today's Deeds

○ QURAN
_____
_____

○ SADAQA
_____
_____

○ DUAS
_____
_____

○ GOOD SPEECH
_____
_____

○ KIND ACTION
_____
_____

○ NIGHT PRAYER
_____
_____

Tomorrow's Ramadan Goal
_____
_____
_____
_____
_____

Quran Study

before		after
start: surah .... ayah .... finish: surah .... ayah	**FAJR**	start: surah .... ayah .... finish: surah .... ayah ....
start: surah .... ayah .... finish: surah .... ayah	**DHUHR**	start: surah .... ayah .... finish: surah .... ayah ....
start: surah .... ayah .... finish: surah .... ayah	**ASR**	start: surah .... ayah .... finish: surah .... ayah ....
start: surah .... ayah .... finish: surah .... ayah	**MAGHRIB**	start: surah .... ayah .... finish: surah .... ayah ....
start: surah .... ayah .... finish: surah .... ayah	**ISHA'A**	start: surah .... ayah .... finish: surah .... ayah ....

Reflection

_____

_____
_____
_____
_____
_____
_____
_____

Applecation

_____

_____
_____
_____
_____
_____

To Do List

- [ ] _____
- [ ] _____
- [ ] _____
- [ ] _____
- [ ] _____
- [ ] _____
- [ ] _____
- [ ] _____

Meal Planner

SAHUR	IFTAR	DINNER

Water Tracker

Adequate Daily Fluid Intake is:

15.5 cups (3.7 liters) a day for men

11.5 cups (2.7 liters) a day for women

Ramadan Day 28

Mood

○ HAPPY   ○ OKAY

○ INSPIRED   ○ TIRED

○ PEACEFUL   ○ ANGRY

Du'a of the Day

رَبَّنَا ٱغْفِرْ لَنَا وَلِإِخْوَٰنِنَا ٱلَّذِينَ سَبَقُونَا بِٱلْإِيمَـٰنِ

وَلَا تَجْعَلْ فِى قُلُوبِنَا غِـلًّا لِّلَّذِينَ ءَامَنُوا۟

رَبَّنَآ إِنَّكَ رَءُوفٌ رَّحِيمٌ

(الحشر:10)

Rabbanā igh'fir lanā wali-ikh'wāninā alladhīna
sabaqūnā bil-īmāni walā taj`al fī qulūbinā
ghillan lilladhīna āmanū rabbanā
innaka raūfun rahīmun

(Al-Hashr 10)

Our Lord! Forgive us and our fellow believers
who preceded us in faith, and do not allow
bitterness into our hearts towards those
who believe. Our Lord! Indeed, You are
Ever Gracious, Most Merciful.

Reflection

_____

_____

_____

_____

_____

_____

_____

Salah Tracker

FAJR
S 2 · F 2

DHUHR
S 4 · F 4 · S 2 · N 2

ASR
S 4 · F 4

MAGHRIB
F 3 · S 2 · N 2

ISHA'A
S 4 · F 4 · S 2 · N 2 · W 3 · N 2

TARAWIH
S 2 · S 2 · S 2 · S 2 · S 2 · S 2 · S 2 · S 2

Today's Deeds

○ QURAN
_____
_____

○ DUAS
_____
_____

○ KIND ACTION
_____
_____

○ SADAQA
_____
_____

○ GOOD SPEECH
_____
_____

○ NIGHT PRAYER
_____
_____

Tomorrow's Ramadan Goal

_____
_____
_____
_____
_____

Quran Study

before		after
start: surah .... ayah .... finish: surah .... ayah	**FAJR**	start: surah .... ayah .... finish: surah .... ayah ....
start: surah .... ayah .... finish: surah .... ayah	**DHUHR**	start: surah .... ayah .... finish: surah .... ayah ....
start: surah .... ayah .... finish: surah .... ayah	**ASR**	start: surah .... ayah .... finish: surah .... ayah ....
start: surah .... ayah .... finish: surah .... ayah	**MAGHRIB**	start: surah .... ayah .... finish: surah .... ayah ....
start: surah .... ayah .... finish: surah .... ayah	**ISHA'A**	start: surah .... ayah .... finish: surah .... ayah ....

Reflection

_____
_____
_____
_____
_____
_____
_____
_____
_____

Applecation

_____
_____
_____
_____
_____

To Do List

- [ ] _____
- [ ] _____
- [ ] _____
- [ ] _____
- [ ] _____
- [ ] _____
- [ ] _____
- [ ] _____

Meal Planner

SAHUR	IFTAR	DINNER

Water Tracker

Adequate Daily Fluid Intake is:

15.5 cups (3.7 liters) a day for men

11.5 cups (2.7 liters) a day for women

Ramadan Day 29

Mood

○ HAPPY ○ OKAY

○ INSPIRED ○ TIRED

○ PEACEFUL ○ ANGRY

Du'a of the Day

رَّبَّنَا عَلَيْكَ تَوَكَّلْنَا وَ إِلَيْكَ أَنَبْنَا وَ إِلَيْكَ ٱلْمَصِيرُ

(المتحنة: 4)

rabbanā ʿalayka tawakkalnā wa-ilayka
anabnā wa-ilayka l-maṣīru

(Al mumtahanah: 8)

Our Lord! In You we trust. And to You we ʿalwaysʾ
turn. And to You is the final return.

Reflection _____

Salah Tracker

FAJR
S 2 · F 2

DHUHR
S 4 · F 4 · S 2 · N 2

ASR
S 4 · F 4

MAGHRIB
F 3 · S 2 · N 2

ISHA'A
S 4 · F 4 · S 2 · N 2 · W 3 · N 2

TARAWIH
S 2 · S 2 · S 2 · S 2 · S 2 · S 2 · S 2 · S 2

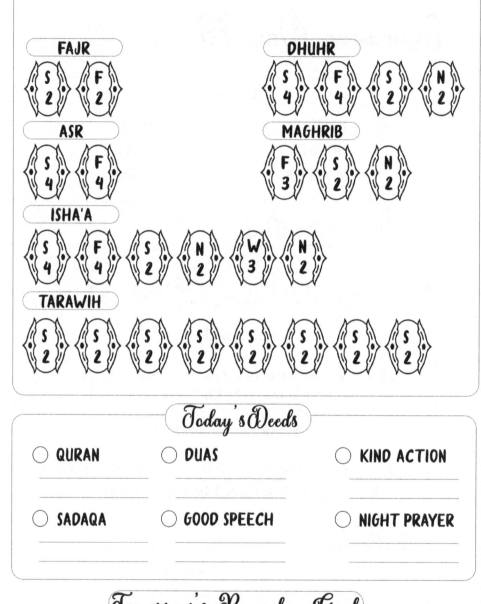

Today's Deeds

- ◯ QURAN
- ◯ DUAS
- ◯ KIND ACTION

- ◯ SADAQA
- ◯ GOOD SPEECH
- ◯ NIGHT PRAYER

Tomorrow's Ramadan Goal

Quran Study

before		after
start: surah .... ayah .... finish: surah .... ayah	**FAJR**	start: surah .... ayah .... finish: surah .... ayah ....
start: surah .... ayah .... finish: surah .... ayah	**DHUHR**	start: surah .... ayah .... finish: surah .... ayah ....
start: surah .... ayah .... finish: surah .... ayah	**ASR**	start: surah .... ayah .... finish: surah .... ayah ....
start: surah .... ayah .... finish: surah .... ayah	**MAGHRIB**	start: surah .... ayah .... finish: surah .... ayah ....
start: surah .... ayah .... finish: surah .... ayah	**ISHA'A**	start: surah .... ayah .... finish: surah .... ayah ....

Reflection

Applecation

To Do List

- [ ] _____
- [ ] _____
- [ ] _____
- [ ] _____
- [ ] _____
- [ ] _____
- [ ] _____
- [ ] _____

Meal Planner

SAHUR	IFTAR	DINNER

Water Tracker

Adequate Daily Fluid Intake is:

15.5 cups (3.7 liters) a day for men

11.5 cups (2.7 liters) a day for women

Ramadan Day 30

Mood

○ HAPPY   ○ OKAY

○ INSPIRED   ○ TIRED

○ PEACEFUL   ○ ANGRY

Du'a of the Day

رَبَّنَا لَا تَجْعَلْنَا فِتْنَةً لِّلَّذِينَ كَفَرُوا وَاغْفِرْ لَنَا رَبَّنَا إِنَّكَ أَنتَ الْعَزِيزُ الْحَكِيمُ

(الممتحنة: 5)

Rabbanā lā taj`alnā fit'natan lilladhīna kafarū
wa-igh'fir lanā rabbanā innaka
anta l-`azīzu l-ĥakīmu

(Al mumtahanah: 5)

Our Lord! Do not subject us to the persecution of
the disbelievers. Forgive us, our Lord!
You ˹alone˺ are truly the Almighty, All-Wise.

Reflection _____

_____

_____

_____

_____

_____

Salah Tracker

FAJR

S 2 — F 2

DHUHR

S 4 — F 4 — S 2 — N 2

ASR

S 4 — F 4

MAGHRIB

F 3 — S 2 — N 2

ISHA'A

S 4 — F 4 — S 2 — N 2 — W 3 — N 2

TARAWIH

S 2 — S 2 — S 2 — S 2 — S 2 — S 2 — S 2 — S 2

Today's Deeds

○ QURAN

○ DUAS

○ KIND ACTION

○ SADAQA

○ GOOD SPEECH

○ NIGHT PRAYER

Tomorrow's Ramadan Goal

Quran Study

before		after
start: surah .... ayah .... finish: surah .... ayah	**FAJR**	start: surah .... ayah .... finish: surah .... ayah ....
start: surah .... ayah .... finish: surah .... ayah	**DHUHR**	start: surah .... ayah .... finish: surah .... ayah ....
start: surah .... ayah .... finish: surah .... ayah	**ASR**	start: surah .... ayah .... finish: surah .... ayah ....
start: surah .... ayah .... finish: surah .... ayah	**MAGHRIB**	start: surah .... ayah .... finish: surah .... ayah ....
start: surah .... ayah .... finish: surah .... ayah	**ISHA'A**	start: surah .... ayah .... finish: surah .... ayah ....

Reflection

_____
_____
_____
_____
_____
_____
_____
_____

Applecation

_____
_____
_____
_____
_____
_____

To Do List

- [ ]
- [ ]
- [ ]
- [ ]

- [ ]
- [ ]
- [ ]
- [ ]

Meal Planner

SAHUR	IFTAR	DINNER

Water Tracker

Adequate Daily Fluid Intake is:

15.5 cups (3.7 liters) a day for men

11.5 cups (2.7 liters) a day for women

يرجى المحافظة على هذا الكتاب وجعله في مكان مناسب ولائق بمكانته لكونه يحتوي على آيات الله سبحانه وتعالى ، والحرص على وضعه في مكان نظيف، وأن لا يوضع على الأرض مباشرة من غير أن يرفع عنها ولو قليلا

إذا كان لديك أي ملاحظات حول هذا الكتاب، يرجى مراسلتنا عبر البريد الإلكتروني

alamaljournals@gmail.com

Please keep this book and make it in a suitable and decent place because it contains the verses of Allah Subhanahu wa ta'ala , and be careful to put it in a clean place, and not put it on the ground directly without lifting it even a little.

If you have any notes about this book, please email us

alamaljournals@gmail.com

Made in the USA
Las Vegas, NV
04 February 2024

85227395R10075